SIMPLE GLASS PAINTING

simple
glass painting

Cheryl Owen

David & Charles

A DAVID & CHARLES BOOK

First published in the UK in 1999
First published in paperback in the UK 2002
Reprinted 2004

Distributed in North America
by F&W Publications, Inc.
4700 E. Galbraith Rd.
Cincinnati, OH 45236
1-800-289-0963

A catalogue record for this book is
available from the British Library.

ISBN 0 7153 1362 2 (paperback)

DESIGNER   *Jane Lanaway*
PHOTOGRAPHER   *Amanda Heywood*

Printed in Italy by LEGO SpA
for David & Charles
Brunel House Newton Abbot Devon

Contents

Introduction

For centuries, the art of making stained glass has produced works of luminous beauty and mystical appeal. Nowadays, the wonderful ranges of glass paints that are available make it possible to imitate the timeless beauty of stained glass on a smaller scale. With painted designs on glass you can capture light, whether natural or artificial, to create magical, sparkling effects. And since light itself is always changing, decorative glass is constantly eyecatching and fascinating, whether it is a painted panel hanging in a sunny window, richly coloured candle-holders for the table or a jewelled ornament on the Christmas tree. Since we all use glass in so many ways, there are countless opportunities for decorating it with colour and pattern, and both the novice and the accomplished painter will find plenty of inspiration in the following pages.

If you are new to this medium but are already a crafts enthusiast, you may discover in glass painting some similarities with the procedures used in, say, silk painting or cake icing. You will also find that, like so many other 'hands-on' hobbies, glass painting has many therapeutic qualities. Glass, with its uniquely beautiful combination of resilience and fluidity, is a wonderful material to work on, while the pure, vivid hues of the paints cannot fail to lift your spirits.

The trace-off templates that accompany each project will enable you to recreate the motifs exactly, or you may prefer to use the designs shown here purely for inspiration to help you create your own. Simply changing the colours used will give a completely different look to a piece, so have fun and experiment – you will find that wonderful results often occur by chance.

Materials

Glass painting is not an expensive hobby to set up if you are starting from scratch.
A little paint goes a long way and you will not need a huge range of colours
initially, as the colours can be mixed to create new shades. Experiment on
expendable glassware such as jam jars or milk bottles before you begin to decorate
a precious piece. Even clear plastic packaging can be used to try out designs.

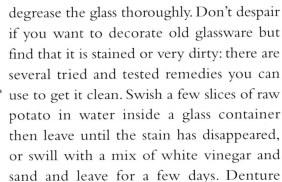

GLASSWARE

Once you start looking for glass with an eye to painting it, you will find endless possibilities. You are bound to have plenty of bottles and jars in the kitchen and bathroom. These can have their labels soaked off in water or removed with a cotton wool pad soaked with nail varnish remover or lighter fuel.

Clear glass is the most versatile, but lovely effects can be achieved on coloured and frosted glass. Faceted pieces are ideal if you are a beginner, as the angles can be traced with outliner before painting, to give a professional-looking result.

Charity and second-hand shops usually have a stock of cheap glassware. Craft shops and mail order craft suppliers stock glassware especially for painting, such as paperweights and suncatchers. Don't forget that you can give recycled glass a new use. For example, a slim oil or vinegar bottle could become an elegant bud vase, and a small, nicely shaped jam jar could have a new life as a pretty votive to hold a nightlight. Before painting, clean and dry all glassware well. Wipe both sides with methylated spirit on a clean, soft cloth to

degrease the glass thoroughly. Don't despair if you want to decorate old glassware but find that it is stained or very dirty: there are several tried and tested remedies you can use to get it clean. Swish a few slices of raw potato in water inside a glass container then leave until the stain has disappeared, or swill with a mix of white vinegar and sand and leave for a few days. Denture cleaner dissolved in hot water may also do the trick.

PLASTICS

Glass-painting techniques can be used very effectively on clear acetate, which is available in various thicknesses from stationers, or art and craft shops. Plastic packaging can also be painted, but always paint a test area first to make sure the plastic is compatible with the paint.

Neoprene foam is a thin, lightweight, plastic foam, which gives a good result when used to make stamps.

Sticky-backed plastic can be used to make stencils and can even be incorporated into the finished design. It adheres well to glass and stops paint seeping underneath when stencilling, but it also peels away easily after use. Stencil sheet can also be used to make stencils for flat pieces, but must be temporarily glued to the glass.

PAPER AND CARD

Kitchen paper is indispensable for cleaning brushes and wiping away errors. When you are painting a round item such as a tumbler, a few sheets under the glass will stop it rolling around. Use tracing paper for templates. It is easy to tape inside glasses and jars, and as it is translucent you will be able to check the design from all angles. If you are going to need to draw around a template more than once, use thick paper or thin card. Use scraps of corrugated card to make backing for foam stamps, and thin coloured card to make greetings cards.

OUTLINER

To imitate stained glass, paint is applied within a raised outline of acrylic paste, piped from a tube. The raised line forms a reservoir to contain the paint. Outliner comes in black, gold, silver and pewter.

PAINTS

Transparent glass paints are available in vivid colours. Most look quite dark in their containers, so you may find it useful to paint a swatch of each colour for reference on a spare sheet of glass or acetate. Both oil-based and water-based glass paints are available: do not mix the two. Crystal gels are water-based, and come in transparent, semi-transparent and iridescent shades. They are quite thick but will liquefy when stirred.

Black and white glass paints are opaque and make any glass paint they are mixed with opaque too. To lighten a colour while retaining its transparency, mix it with colourless paint. Ceramic paints are semi-transparent or opaque, and work well on glass.

Frosted and crackle-glazed effects can be produced using special media. Painted items can be varnished if you wish: this will give protection and make the colours light-fast, but can dull the paint.

Most painted glass can be washed carefully in warm, soapy water then gently buffed to a shine, but you should leave a newly painted piece for at least a week before washing it for the first time. Some paints can be hardened by baking the finished pieces in a domestic oven: check the paint manufacturer's instructions. Generally, a painted surface should not come into contact with food.

If you are painting glassware as a gift, allow plenty of time for it to dry thoroughly, then pack it well in lots of tissue paper. Do not use plastic bubble wrap as the bubbles may become imprinted on the paint surface.

ADHESIVE LEAD STRIP

This is available on reels from DIY stores. It usually comes with a boning peg, which is the tool used to stick the strip smoothly to the glass. While you are working with lead strip, do not smoke or handle food, and always keep the lead well out of reach of children. Wash your hands thoroughly after use.

EMBELLISHMENTS

Glue jewellery stones, glass nuggets or sequins to the painted pieces for added sparkle, using superglue or PVA adhesive. You can build up a collection of suitable material, hoarding fragments of broken jewellery and other small treasures whenever you find them.

Equipment

You probably already have most of the equipment you will need for glass painting, as no special tools are required. For comfort and safety, work on a flat, clean surface, keeping glass, paints and sharp implements beyond the reach of children. Old plastic carrier bags, cut open and laid flat, will give water-repellent protection to the surface underneath.

DRAWING TOOLS

A propelling pencil or sharp HB pencil is best for drawing. Use a pencil or dark-coloured felt-tipped pen when making templates. For accuracy, use a ruler or set square to draw squares and rectangles, and a pair of compasses to describe a circle. Measure curved surfaces with a tape measure. A chinagraph pencil gives a waxy line which works well on glass and can be wiped away easily.

CUTTING TOOLS

Cut paper and plastics with a pair of scissors or a craft knife. Always use a craft knife on a cutting mat and replace the blade regularly as a blunt blade will not cut smoothly and may tear paper. Use metal cutters or an old pair of scissors to cut lead. When working with acetate, make holes for hanging with a hole punch, the point of a scissor blade or a thick needle, depending upon the size of hole you need.

PAINTING TOOLS AND ACCESSORIES

Glass paint can be used straight from the containers, but if you need to mix the colours, use a white ceramic tile, an old plate or a paint tray.

Curved glassware needs to be supported while it is being painted: sitting a piece on a reel of tape often works well, or balancing the rim on an eraser may sometimes be enough to support the glass. To prevent paint running, work only on the uppermost area, allow to dry a little, then turn the glass to continue.

Masking tape is ideal for attaching templates, and masking off areas not to be painted. If you are using a stencil sheet, attach it temporarily using spray adhesive.

Use good quality artist's paintbrushes and clean them well after use. A fine paintbrush is useful for getting into tight corners of the outlined shape, while a flat paintbrush will give good coverage over a large area. A stencil brush is recommended for stencilling and stippling. Use natural or synthetic sponges for a mottled effect. Cotton buds can be useful for wiping off small amounts of paint. Use a hair dryer, on its lowest setting, held at approximately 15cm/6in from the work, to help dry the paint.

Always clean your paintbrushes immediately after use. If you are using oil-based paints, clean brushes with white spirit or a thinner recommended by the paint manufacturer. Clean brushes with water and detergent if you are using water-based paints.

Designs and Templates

Trace-off templates accompany the projects in this book. To use one of these, place a piece of tracing paper over the design and trace it with a sharp pencil or pen, then roughly cut round the shape.

DOUBLE CURVATURES

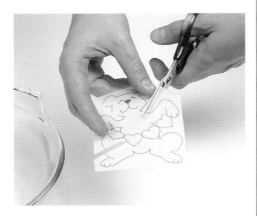

1 Templates to be used on rounded glassware will need to be adapted to fit the curves. Make cuts into the template.

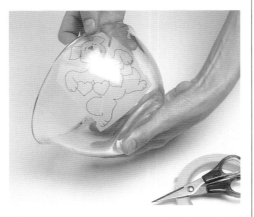

2 Slip the template under the glass and tape it in place at the top and bottom. The cuts will overlap or spread open to fit the curves of the glassware.

STRAIGHT-SIDED CONTAINERS

1 The sides of many straight-sided containers are not as parallel as they may appear. To make a template, slip a piece of tracing paper into the container. Adjust the position of the paper so that it lies smoothly against the glass. Tape in place and mark the position of the overlap and the upper edge with a pencil.

2 Remove the tracing and join up the overlap marks. Measure down from the upper edge and mark the upper limit of the decoration on the template. Join the marks to create an outline within which to fit your motifs. Cut out and slip the template into the container to check the fit, adjusting it if necessary.

ENLARGING AND REDUCING DESIGNS

1 Use a photocopier for fast and accurate results if you need to enlarge or reduce a design. Measure the width of the image you want to end up with. This shell motif, for example, needs to be enlarged to 50mm to fit a raised surface on a jam jar. Measure the width of the original image, which in this case is 36mm. Divide the first measurement by the second to find the percentage by which you need to enlarge the image, in this case 139%.

2 Trace the new image and check the fit. Remember that an enlargement must always be more than 100% and a reduction less than 100%.

CREATING BACKGROUND DESIGNS

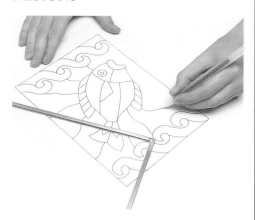

It is easier to apply glass paints within a small outliner reservoir than within a large area. When creating your own designs, divide any large areas into smaller sections. This is especially relevant when painting extensive background areas.

POSITIONING MOTIFS

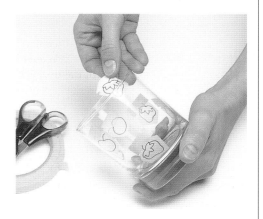

If you draw your templates on tracing paper, you will be able to see how they look from all viewpoints. When positioning more than one motif inside glassware, check from all angles to see how the motifs look together. When you are positioning motifs on a glass that will be drunk from, place them at least 2cm/³⁄₄in below the rim to avoid contact with the lips.

DRAWING AROUND A TEMPLATE

1 It is not always possible to trace a template through glassware. The glass may be frosted or coloured, it may be very thick or have a small opening. If you simply need an outline, you can trace it onto tracing paper with a pencil. Tape the tracing face down onto paper – cartridge paper, for example – and redraw the image. Use thin card instead of paper if you will need to use the template more than once.

2 Cut out the template. Tape or hold it against the glass and draw around the image. Use a chinagraph pencil on clear glass or draw lightly with a sharp lead pencil on frosted glass.

CHINAGRAPH PENCIL TRANSFER

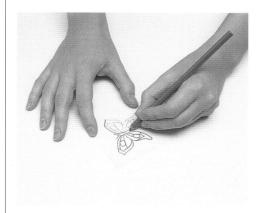

1 To transfer detailed templates, trace the image onto tracing paper. Turn the tracing over and redraw the lines with a chinagraph pencil. Chinagraph pencils are prone to blunt quickly, but it doesn't matter if the lines are thick and heavy.

2 Tape the template, chinagraph pencil side down, on the glass. Draw over the lines again with a sharp pencil to transfer the design to the glass.

The Outliner

Different brands of outliner handle differently and are affected in various ways by temperature and humidity. It is best to test the flow of the outliner before you start each application. If it has dried inside the nozzle, push a pin into the end to unblock it.

APPLYING OUTLINER

Lean forward so you are looking down on the work and can see the design clearly. Squeeze the tube gently as you draw it along the outline. The outliner almost always starts with a blob! Don't worry – it can be neatened when it has dried. When working on three-dimensional pieces, work on the uppermost area, leave to dry, then turn the object to continue. Wipe the nozzle on kitchen paper and replace the lid when you have finished, to prevent the outliner from drying out.

SPEED DRYING

Generally, outliner takes about 10 minutes to set hard. Use a hair dryer on its lowest setting to dry outliner or paint quickly.

TRACING WATER LEVEL

To apply level lines of outliner around a container, stand it on a level surface and fill to the lowest level needed, then trace around the water level with the outliner. Add more water to apply higher lines.

NEATENING MISTAKES

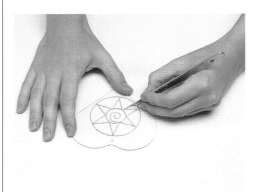

Wipe away any major mistakes before the outliner has dried. Leave to dry then check to see if any areas could be improved; bear in mind that once the piece is painted, the eye will be drawn to the painted areas rather than the outline. Cut away the edges of any blobs with a craft knife. Do not neaten the line too much or it will appear to have been created by machine and lose its handcrafted look, but a more professional appearance can be achieved by tidying up some irregularities in the line.

Basic Painting

Most transparent glass paints available today are oil-based and can give off quite strong fumes, so be sure to work in a well ventilated environment. When painting clear glass, work on a white surface: just slip a piece of white paper under the work so you can see the paint clearly.

PAINTING WITHIN THE OUTLINER

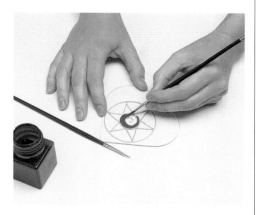

Apply the paint generously, using a fine paintbrush to poke it into tight corners of the outliner. Distribute the paint evenly over the surface of the glass. Hold the glass up to the light from time to time to check that it is not patchy and that it has reached the inner edges of the outliner.

BLENDING COLOURS

To create a new colour, mix two colours together on a white ceramic tile, old plate or mixing tray. Clean the paintbrush well when changing colours then stir the two colours together on the tile. To blend colours on the glass to create shading, apply them separately to the glass then blend together within the outliner. To avoid dirtying paints in their containers, put the various colours on the tile before mixing and pick them up with a paintbrush from there.

USING CERAMIC PAINTS

Use ceramic paints if you want a dense, opaque colouring. The effect will be bolder than with transparent glass paints.

PAINTING WITHOUT OUTLINER

If there is no outliner to hold the paint, do not apply it too thickly or it will run. Just build up the colour gradually.

Paint Effects

Once you feel confident handling glass paint, you can experiment with different techniques and methods of application to introduce interesting textures into your designs. The effects described here are used in some of the projects shown in the book.

WET-ON-WET PAINT

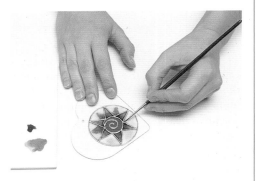

Lovely soft effects can be created by painting onto wet paint. Use a fine paintbrush and apply a different colour over the area you have just painted. Do not blend the colours; they will spread a little naturally. Leave to dry.

ETCHING

Etch simple, quirky designs into wet paint. Use a flat paintbrush or a sponge to apply the paint then draw on the surface with a clean fine paintbrush or cotton bud. To keep the design neat, wipe the excess paint off the brush after each stroke.

STIPPLING

Hold a paintbrush upright to dab paint in a pouncing motion onto the glass. A stencil brush is the best shape to use for stippling, although a smaller brush can be used for tight areas. Do not pick up too much paint with the brush, and dab off any excess on kitchen paper before you begin.

WET-ON-DRY PAINT

Leave a painted area to dry then paint on top to add detail. Avoid giving a whole area a second coat of paint however, as it will dissolve the first coat.

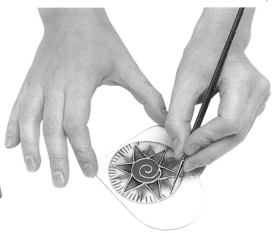

SPONGING WITH NATURAL SPONGE

A random, mottled effect can be created quickly using a natural sponge. Moisten the sponge with white spirit or water, depending on the paint you are using. Dab off the excess moisture on kitchen paper. Apply the paint to a tile. Dab at the paint with the sponge then dab it onto the glass.

SPONGING WITH SYNTHETIC SPONGE

A synthetic sponge can be used in the same way as a natural sponge. The resulting effect will be more uniform in style.

DECORATING WITH A FROSTING MEDIUM

The frosting medium used here is mixed with glass and tile paint made by the same manufacturer to produce a delicate, cloudy effect. Read the instructions on the frosting medium carefully before you use it, as some makes need to be applied on top of a surface that is already painted.

PAINTING ON FROSTED GLASS

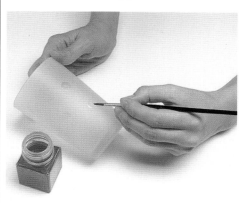

If you paint frosted glass with transparent glass paint, it will become clear. Keep the designs simple, and use colourless paint to give a high quality, etched effect.

CRYSTAL GEL

Squeeze the gel from the tube onto a ceramic tile, old plate or paint tray. If you stir the gel well it will liquefy, and can be applied with a paintbrush. If you prefer, use the gel straight from the tube for a thick, lumpy effect. It can also be applied with a palette knife.

CRACKLE GLAZE

Some crackle glaze is compatible with certain glass paints, but read the glaze manufacturer's instructions before application, as the method of use may vary. Paint the crackle glaze onto paint that has dried completely. The more thickly the glaze is applied, the wider the cracks will be. Set aside to dry and cracks will gradually appear.

VARNISHING

If you wish, paint a coat of gloss or matt varnish over the painted design, applying the varnish just over the outer edges of the outliner. Bear in mind that although the varnish dries clear and will protect the design, it will dull the paint colours.

Stencilling

Stencilling works well on glassware, but it is generally best to use ceramic paints as they will show up more than transparent glass paints, unless the latter are mixed with white. Allow the paints to dry before peeling off the stencils.

STENCILLING USING MASKING TAPE

Mask off areas with masking tape to create a smooth, level edge for your painting. This works well for stripes and geometric shapes. Follow a template or measure the glass to position the tape, and smooth along the edges to ensure a good seal so that paint does not seep underneath.

STENCILLING USING STICKY-BACKED PLASTIC

1 Trace the design onto tracing paper. Go over the lines on the underside of the tracing with a soft pencil. Tape the tracing right side up onto the paper backing of a piece of sticky-backed plastic. Redraw to transfer the image. Cut out with a craft knife on a cutting mat.

2 Place the stencil on the glass. Starting at one edge, gradually peel off the backing paper and stick the stencil smoothly onto the glass.

USING A STENCIL SHEET

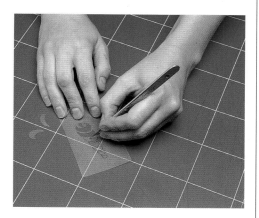

1 A stencil sheet can also be used to stencil on glass. Trace the design onto the stencil sheet with a pen. Cut out the design using a craft knife on a cutting mat.

2 As the surfaces of glass and the stencil sheet are both shiny, they will not adhere together and paint will seep under the stencil, so it must be glued to the glass temporarily. Lightly coat the underside of the stencil with spray adhesive. Stick to the glass. After painting, peel off the stencil and carefully clean any glue residue from the glass. Do a test piece first to make sure that paint is not removed too.

APPLYING THE PAINT

1 Apply a thin film of paint to a ceramic tile or an old plate, using a flat paintbrush. Holding a stencil brush upright, dab at the paint to pick up a small amount at a time. Hold the brush upright to dab the paint through the holes in the stencil, moving the brush with a circular motion. Leave to dry before stencilling another colour on top.

2 Best results are achieved with a stencil brush when stencilling small cut-outs, but an ordinary brush can be used for larger areas. Use a flat paintbrush to apply the paint evenly.

3 Another way of stencilling is to use a sponge, either natural or synthetic. Moisten the sponge with white spirit if you are using oil-based paints or with water if you are using water-based paints. Squeeze out any excess moisture on kitchen paper. Apply a thin film of paint to a ceramic tile or an old plate, using a flat paintbrush. Dab at the paint with the sponge then apply the sponge lightly through the stencil. Clean the sponge immediately after use.

REVERSE STENCILLING

In this case, paint is applied to the area surrounding a stencil rather than the space within it. Use a template to cut your chosen shape from sticky-backed plastic. Peel off the backing paper and stick the motif to the glass. Paint the glass, painting over the stencil with a stencil brush, ordinary paintbrush or sponge. Leave to dry then peel off the stencil to reveal the unpainted glass underneath.

Stamping

Stamping is a quick and easy way to produce repeated designs on flat pieces of glass. You can buy ready-made stamps from craft suppliers, but it is not difficult to cut out your own designs. Make some test prints on a spare sheet of glass to check how much paint you need to apply.

MAKING YOUR OWN STAMP

1 Draw the template on paper. Cut it out and draw around it on a piece of neoprene foam. Cut out with a craft knife or a pair of scissors. Stick the foam shape to a piece of corrugated card, using all-purpose household glue.

2 Cut the card around the foam, leaving a margin of 5mm/¼in. The card margin will enable you to hold the stamp without smudging the paint and will act as a guide for positioning.

3 Apply a thin film of paint to a ceramic tile or an old plate and press the stamp firmly onto the paint to pick up an even coating. Alternatively, apply an even coat of paint directly onto the stamp using a paintbrush. Experiment with both methods to see which one gives you the best result.

4 Press the stamp firmly onto the glass then lift it off. Reapply the paint before stamping the next motif. Wipe the stamp clean before changing colours and immediately after use.

5 Stamps can also be cut from synthetic sponge. A kitchen sponge backed with a scourer makes a good stamp and is widely available. Draw the design on the scourer side of the sponge, drawing around a template if necessary. Cut out the design using a craft knife. Do not use scissors to cut the thick sponge as they will distort the design.

Acetate

Apply outliner and paint to acetate in the same way as when decorating glass. Use masking tape to stick templates temporarily in position. If you need to neaten the outliner, do so sparingly and carefully, as a knife blade can leave scratch marks on the acetate.

CUTTING ACETATE

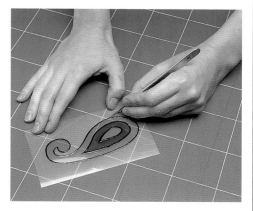

Cut acetate with a craft knife or a pair of scissors. A craft knife will give a neater result when cutting curves on thick acetate. If you are cutting intricately shaped pieces, paint the acetate first, then allow it to dry before cutting. Use the craft knife on a cutting mat, and do not try to cut all the way through with the first stroke, but gradually cut deeper and deeper.

MAKING HOLES

1 Use a hole punch to make a hole if it needs to be large enough to thread with thick cord or several strands of raffia.

2 Use the point of a scissor blade or a thick needle to make a small hole in the acetate to suspend it from thread, fine cord or narrow ribbon. Lay the acetate on a cutting mat or scrap of thick card and pierce through into the surface underneath. Pick up the acetate and work the point around in the hole to enlarge it.

FOLDING FINE ACETATE

Fine acetate is flexible enough to fold to make three-dimensional shapes, such as the gift bags on page 92. Cut the acetate to size, decorate it, then weight or tape it face down on a template. Fold the acetate along the foldlines on the template.

Adhesive Lead Strip

Flexible lead strips can be used to imitate the joints between panels of stained glass. As adhesive lead is stuck onto the surface of the glass, it looks most effective in situations where it is viewed from the front only, such as on a mirror.

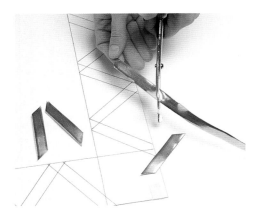

1 Tape a template for a leading design under the glass or draw the design on a mirror using a chinagraph pencil. Starting with the shortest length needed, cut a piece of lead slightly shorter at each end than the length of the line you wish to cover, using a pair of metal cutters or a craft knife on a cutting mat.

2 Peel off the backing tape. Stick the lead to the glass, taking care not to stretch the lead or to touch the adhesive.

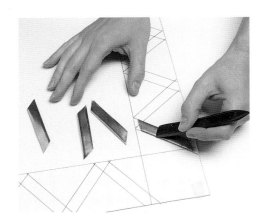

3 Run the concave end of the boning peg along the centre of the lead.

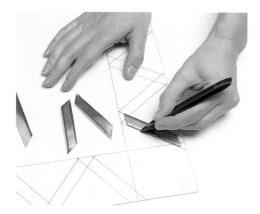

4 Now hold the pointed end of the boning peg at a 45° angle, leaning towards the lead. Run the peg smoothly along each edge to stick the strip to the glass.

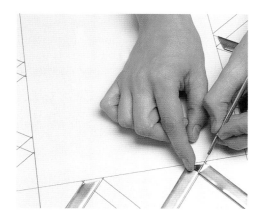

5 Apply more strips, gradually building up the design. Where two strips overlap and a third strip is to cover the junction, cut the second strip with a craft knife where it touches the first strip.

6 Apply longer pieces of lead to cover the ends of the short strips, starting and finishing 5mm/¼in inside the outer edges if these will be covered by more lead. Smooth down using the boning peg.

7 Finally, paint the panels within the leaded design, using glass paints as you would within a perimeter of outliner. If any paint seeps onto the lead, wipe it away immediately while it is still wet.

Embellishments

Finishing touches such as glass nuggets and 'jewels' can be used as focal points in a design, to enhance the shape of a piece, or just to provide extra sparkle and decorative detail. Apply jewellery stones to the glass before you paint the rest of the design.

STICKING ON JEWELLERY STONES

Glue jewellery stones to glass using superglue, if the glass is to be washed occasionally, or PVA glue if the piece is purely decorative.

APPLYING STICKY-BACKED PLASTIC SHAPES

Small shapes cut from sticky-backed plastic, especially metallic-effect plastic, work well with many designs. Simply cut out the shape, peel off the backing paper and stick smoothly in place.

ADDING OUTLINER ON TOP OF PAINT

Outliner can be applied to painted glass as a highlight. Keep the application simple: dots added at random or in patterns are very effective. Replace a template under a piece painted with transparent glass paints to use as a guide if necessary.

OUTLINING EMBELLISHMENTS

After attaching a jewellery stone or sticky-backed plastic shape, edge it with outliner to fill the gap between it and the glass, as this will prevent paint seeping underneath and will cover any excess glue.

APPLYING SEQUINS

Use PVA glue to stick sequins to painted glassware. A pair of tweezers is very useful for holding and positioning them.

Trouble-shooting

The step-by-step instructions and photographs that accompany the designs in this book should help you achieve satisfying results. If you are new to glass painting, try out the techniques on some spare pieces of glass until you feel confident about handling the materials. Here are a few tips to help you with some common problems.

GETTING RID OF AIR BUBBLES AND FLUFF

Air bubbles sometimes appear in the paint when you are applying it. Wait for a minute or two before piercing the bubbles with a pin to burst them. Tiny pieces of fluff can be carefully lifted off the wet paint using a pin.

PAINT NOT REACHING OUTLINER

If you notice after the paint has dried that it has not reached the outliner, do not add more paint as this will give a noticeable ridge. Nor should you add a second coat of paint because it will dissolve the first layer. It is best just to add a little more outliner to cover the area where paint is missing.

PAINT ON OUTLINER

If paint has been applied too thickly within the outliner perimeter, it may seep on top of the outliner. To remedy this, either wipe the wet paint off the outliner using a paint-brush or cotton bud, or wait for the paint to dry then scrape it off with a craft knife.

REMOVING PAINT

If you have applied paint in the wrong place, you can lift it off immediately, while still wet, using a paintbrush. Scrape off dried paint and outliner using a craft knife. Clean the glass: a cotton bud dipped in a compatible solvent will pick up any remaining debris. Do not remove dry paint and outliner in this way from acetate and other plastics, as the knife blade will leave scratches on the surface.

The
Projects

Hot-air Balloon Pitcher

THE BULBOUS SHAPE of this glass pitcher suggested

a theme for its decoration: colourful hot-air balloons

floating amongst the clouds. The brilliant colours and

translucent material used to make hot-air balloons make

them very suitable subjects for glass painting. Pewter

outliner is used to draw the sections of the balloons to

give a strong sense of form. The base of the pitcher has

been painted with a simple, undulating landscape of hazy

green hills. Finally, a few light touches from a natural

sponge between the balloons suggest the merest

wisps of white clouds on a bright, summer's day.

Materials & Equipment

TRACING PAPER

PENCIL

SCISSORS

CLEAR GLASS PITCHER

MASKING TAPE

GLASS PAINTS: OLIVE GREEN, BRIGHT GREEN, TURQUOISE, BRIGHT PINK, LEMON YELLOW, PALE PINK, BRIGHT BLUE AND PALE BLUE

FLAT, MEDIUM AND FINE PAINTBRUSHES

WHITE CERAMIC TILE, OLD PLATE OR MIXING TRAY

KITCHEN PAPER

PEWTER OUTLINER

CRAFT KNIFE

SMALL NATURAL SPONGE

WHITE SPIRIT OR WATER

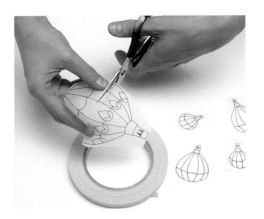

1 Trace one large and two each of the small balloons onto tracing paper and cut them out roughly. If your pitcher has a curved surface like this one, make two cuts into the side edges of the large balloon tracing. Slip the tracing inside the pitcher and stick it smoothly in place at the top and bottom with masking tape. The cuts will overlap to fit the curved shape.

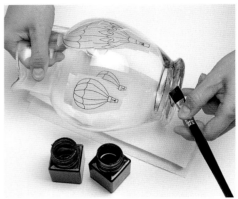

2 Stick the small balloon tracings under the glass. You may need to snip them in the same way as the large tracing to make them lie smoothly. To make the landscape at the base of the pitcher, paint simple curved hill shapes in olive green paint. While the paint is still wet, paint more hills on top as if they are in the foreground, using bright green paint. Take care not to apply the paint too thickly or it may run. Leave to dry.

4 Paint the balloons, allowing the uppermost areas to dry before turning the pitcher to continue.

3 Draw the balloons using the outliner. Use outliner to fill in the people in the balloon baskets. Leave to dry. Check that the outliner 'ropes' do not appear too thick, and carefully neaten them with a craft knife if necessary.

5 Apply a little pale blue and bright blue paint to a white ceramic tile or plate. Lightly moisten a small, natural sponge with white spirit, if you are using oil-based paints, or water, if you are using water-based paints. Dab at the paint with the sponge then gently dab the sponge onto the pitcher to form a few clouds between the balloons.

Celtic Whisky Tumblers

WHISKY'S CELTIC ASSOCIATIONS inspired the decoration of this set of tumblers and glass coasters. The tumblers are painted with the distinctive interlaced animal forms that are characteristic of this remarkable style of decoration, in which natural, serpentine shapes are woven into an intricate formal design that fills the available space. There are two designs to choose from. The coaster echoes the style with a more abstract pattern. The decoration can be given an extra dimension by careful shading, so that the twists and turns of the shapes really appear to be passing over and under each other. The colours have also been inspired by the subtle honey and amber tones of different whiskies, accented by gold outliner.

Materials & Equipment

TRACING PAPER

PENCIL

SCISSORS

CLEAR GLASS TUMBLERS
AND COASTERS

MASKING TAPE

KITCHEN PAPER

GOLD OUTLINER

GLASS PAINTS: LIGHT AND
DEEP BROWN, ORANGE,
LIGHT AND DEEP YELLOW

WHITE CERAMIC TILE,
OLD PLATE OR MIXING TRAY

PAINTBRUSH

1 Trace the tumbler and coaster motifs onto tracing paper and cut around them. Check the fit inside the glass: the tumbler tracing is designed to meet edge to edge along the broken lines. Tape the tumbler tracing inside the tumbler, at least 2cm/¾in below the rim. Lay the tumbler on its side on a few sheets of kitchen paper and trace along the outline with gold outliner. Leave to dry, then turn the tumbler to continue tracing the design.

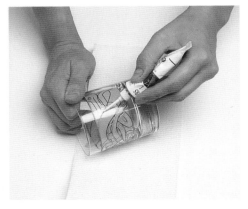

2 Remove the tracing and paint the design. Remember to paint a complete section before moving on to the next one, and apply deeper shades of a colour where the design appears to go under another section. Work on only the uppermost areas, allow to dry, then turn the tumbler to continue painting.

3 Paint the background area around the design in deep yellow. Leave to dry.

4 As the coaster design is placed around the circumference, cut out the centre of the tracing and tape it under the glass.

5 Turn the coaster over and trace the outline with gold outliner. Leave to dry and remove the tracing.

6 Paint the design. As before, apply darker shades of the colour where the design appears to go under another section. Do not paint the background of the coaster. Set aside to dry.

Paisley Bowl

TRADITIONAL PAISLEY SHAPES have been given a contemporary feel on this beautiful shallow bowl by adding frosting medium to the paints. Details applied with silver outliner accentuate the curves of the basic motif, and the finishing touches are glittering cabuchon crystal jewellery stones. These are applied first and outlined in silver so that they are well integrated with the rest of the design. Follow the paint manufacturer's instructions when applying frosting medium: some types are not mixed with the paint but are applied separately after the paint has dried. You will probably need to make a template to fit your own bowl: see how to do this on page 12. Trace around the paisley shapes within your template outline.

Materials & Equipment

30CM/12IN DIAMETER CLEAR GLASS BOWL

TAPE MEASURE

CHINAGRAPH PENCIL

TRACING PAPER

PENCIL

SCISSORS

MASKING TAPE

SUPER GLUE

7MM/$^5/_{16}$IN DIAMETER CRYSTAL JEWELLERY STONES

SILVER OUTLINER

GLASS PAINTS: BLUE, TURQUOISE AND WHITE

MEDIUM PAINTBRUSH

WHITE CERAMIC TILE, OLD PLATE OR MIXING TRAY

KITCHEN PAPER

FROSTING MEDIUM

1 Divide the circumference of the bowl into quarters and mark with a chinagraph pencil. Enlarge then trace the template onto tracing paper and cut it out. Tape it under the first section. Using superglue, stick a jewellery stone at each dot – dab the glue onto the bowl then position the stone on top. You may need to support the bowl at an angle to stop the glue running.

2 Outline the design with silver outliner. Do not apply outliner along the broken lines at this stage. Leave to dry, then remove the tracing and move it on to the next section. Repeat all around the bowl. Neaten any irregularities in the outline using a craft knife.

3 Paint the paisley shapes blue and turquoise, adding the frosting medium according to the manufacturer's instructions.

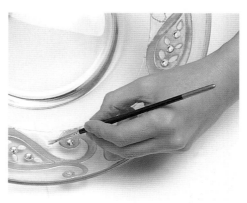

4 Paint the background and small details white, again adding frosting medium. Leave to dry.

5 Tape the tracing under the glass again and apply dots of silver outliner along the broken lines. Move the tracing and repeat in the other sections.

Summer Fruit Glasses

THESE FRUITY GLASSES, with their frosted finish, are perfect for long, iced drinks on hot summer afternoons. The subtle stripes were created by applying colourless glass paint to frosted glass, which makes the surface almost clear. Succulent cherries and strawberries have been painted in rows to complete the decoration, as they are evocative symbols of high summer, but you might like to add other fruit designs of your own, painting each glass with a different fruit, or mixing the motifs together.

Spiral Plates

A REVERSE STENCILLING technique is used to create the swirls and spirals on these dramatic glass plates. The painting couldn't be simpler, and the sharply defined design is revealed as if by magic after the paint has dried. Brightly coloured ceramic paints are used to give density of colour and to show off the shapes. These plates were intended to be used purely for decoration, and have an embossed trademark in the centre, so the painting was done on the top surface to hide it. If you want to be able to eat off your plates, paint them on the underside instead, so that the decorated surface is not in direct contact with food.

Materials & Equipment

CLEAR GLASS PLATES

CHINAGRAPH PENCIL

TRACING PAPER

PENCIL

THIN CARD

SCISSORS

STICKY-BACKED PLASTIC

MASKING TAPE

CERAMIC PAINTS: ORANGE,
RED, MAGENTA, PINK,
TURQUOISE AND BLUE

FLAT PAINTBRUSH

WHITE CERAMIC TILE,
OLD PLATE OR MIXING TRAY

KITCHEN PAPER

1 If your plate does not have a clearly defined rim, draw a line for reference using a chinagraph pencil on the side which is not to be painted. Trace the motifs and transfer them onto thin card. Cut out the templates and draw around each one several times on the paper backing of the sticky-backed plastic.

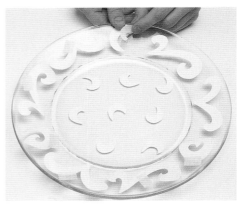

2 Cut out the motifs and arrange them on the plate, placing the larger pieces around the rim. Tape them lightly in place if they slide about. When you are happy with the arrangement, peel off the backing paper and stick the pieces in position.

4 Leave to dry, then paint the rim a different colour. When adding more paint, try to begin the brush stroke on a motif so it will not be obvious on the finished plate.

3 Starting at the centre and working outwards to the inner edge of the rim, use a flat paintbrush to paint an increasing spiral. Hold the brush almost flat against the glass when adding more paint.

5 Leave to dry, then carefully peel off the plastic motifs to reveal the clear glass underneath. If the ceramic paints you have used can be hardened in the oven, follow the manufacturer's instructions to bake them, which will make them very durable.

Leaf and Flower Bowls

THE QUIRKY, naïve decorations on these

colourful bowls are very easy and quick to achieve.

The best position for the designs depends on the style

of the bowls you are using. Place the motifs on the

inside edge of a shallow, open bowl but on the outside

of a high-sided container. The squares are stamped with

a sponge and the motifs are etched in the wet paint.

Opaque ceramic paints are best, so that the contrasting

blocks show up boldly against the strong colours of the

bowls. Refer to the templates when drawing the

motifs, or create your own designs. Either way, the

etching technique is most effective if you keep

the little drawings very simple and spontaneous.

Materials & Equipment

PENCIL

SYNTHETIC SPONGE

CRAFT KNIFE

CUTTING MAT

TAPE MEASURE

GLASS BOWLS IN BLUE
AND GREEN

CHINAGRAPH PENCIL

CERAMIC PAINT: TURQUOISE
AND GOLD

FLAT AND FINE PAINTBRUSHES

WHITE CERAMIC TILE,
OLD PLATE OR MIXING TRAY

KITCHEN PAPER

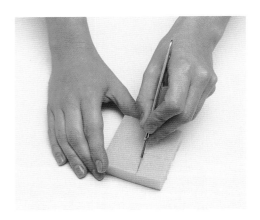

1 Draw a 2.5cm/1in square on the sponge and cut it out with a craft knife. If you are using a kitchen sponge backed with a hard scourer, cut from the underside.

3 Press the sponge onto the bowl between the divisions, applying a firm pressure. Lift off the sponge.

4 While the paint is still wet, use a fine paintbrush to draw a simple leaf or flower motif within the square. Wipe the excess paint off the brush after each stroke.

2 Measure the rim of a bowl and divide it into eight sections, marking the divisions on the glass with a chinagraph pencil. Paint the surface of the sponge with ceramic paint.

5 Continue applying the squares and drawing within them. Set the bowl aside to dry. Wipe away the pencil marks. If the ceramic paints you have used can be hardened in the oven, and the glassware is suitable for this, follow the manufacturer's instructions to bake the bowls, which will make them extra durable.

Clematis
Decanter

WHEN USED WITHOUT OUTLINER, the transparency
of glass paint can be exploited to give a subtle,
impressionistic effect. Natural forms work very well,
and this decanter has been covered in a delicate tracery
of clematis flowers. The flowers are painted freehand to
give them a fragile and handmade quality. The colours
have been chosen to mix harmoniously as they are seen
through the glass, with a few touches of gold to provide
gentle accents. Do not be apprehensive about painting
freehand on glass if you have not tried it before.
Any irregularities in the flowers will simply
add to their natural appearance.

Materials & Equipment

CLEAR GLASS DECANTER

FINE AND MEDIUM PAINTBRUSHES

GLASS PAINTS: OLIVE GREEN, ROSE PINK, ORANGE, DEEP YELLOW AND LEMON YELLOW

WHITE CERAMIC TILE, OLD PLATE OR MIXING TRAY

THICK PAPER (OPTIONAL)

PENCIL (OPTIONAL)

SCISSORS (OPTIONAL)

CHINAGRAPH PENCIL (OPTIONAL)

COTTON BUDS (OPTIONAL)

GOLD OUTLINER

1 Paint a small circle of olive green to form the centre of a flower. Paint six pointed petals radiating outwards from the centre, using either rose pink, orange or deep yellow paint. If you do not feel confident about painting freehand, copy or trace and cut out the template from thick paper and draw around it lightly with a chinagraph pencil onto the glass. Gently rub away the pencil, using cotton buds, as you paint.

2 Cover the surface of the glass with flowers, using the three different colours in turn. Leave to dry then paint olive green leaves between the flowers.

4 Hold a paintbrush upright to stipple lemon yellow paint in a pouncing movement onto any areas of unpainted glass to complete the design.

3 With a fine paintbrush, apply olive green paint in short strokes, radiating out from the flower centres, for the stamens. Dot the flower centres lightly with gold outliner.

5 Starting at the centre top of the stopper, use a fine paintbrush to paint a spiral with olive green paint.

Tex-Mex Mugs

GIVE SOUTHWESTERN STYLE to a pair of chunky

glass mugs by dotting them with some classic Tex-Mex

motifs: fat red chillies, giant cactus plants and a beaming

sun. Ceramic paints, which are semi-opaque, have been

used to give substance to these robust designs in bright,

assertive colours. However, if you prefer, you can define

the motifs with outliner and fill the shapes with glass

paints for a transparent effect. As always, when planning

a design around a glass vessel, consider how the motifs

will look in relation to one another as you see them

through the glass. Don't position them too

close to the rim as the painted surface should

not come into contact with the lips.

Materials & Equipment

TRACING PAPER

PENCIL

SCISSORS

MASKING TAPE

CLEAR GLASS MUGS

CERAMIC PAINTS: GREEN,
TURQUOISE, RED AND YELLOW

MEDIUM AND FINE PAINTBRUSHES

WHITE CERAMIC TILE,
OLD PLATE OR MIXING TRAY

KITCHEN PAPER

1 Trace the motifs a few times onto tracing paper and cut them out roughly. Tape the motifs at random under the glass. Lay the mug on its side, resting it on a support such as a large tape reel to stop it rolling around while you paint. Paint the cacti green or turquoise. Paint the chillies red. Paint a red circle for the sun, and add a dot in the centre. Use a fine paintbrush to paint the sun's rays radiating outwards.

2 Leave to dry, then turn the mug to continue painting the motifs. Use a fine paintbrush to paint the chilli stalks green. Leave to dry, then remove the tracings.

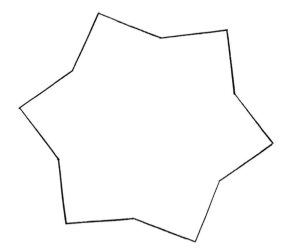

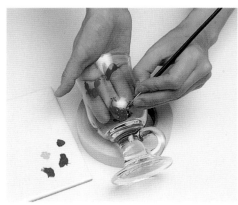

4 Paint yellow spines on the cacti and turquoise wrinkles on the chillies.

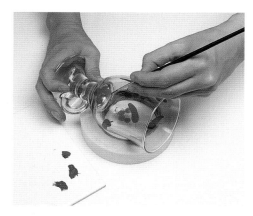

3 Use a fine paintbrush to paint flowers on the cacti – use three short strokes for each flower. Here, red flowers were added to the turquoise cacti and turquoise flowers to the green cacti.

5 If your mugs have stems, trace the zig-zag ring onto tracing paper and tape it under the base. Paint the zig-zags turquoise or green. Paint a matching zig-zag freehand on the handle to finish, then set the mugs aside to dry. If the ceramic paints you have used can be hardened in the oven, follow the manufacturer's instructions to bake them, which will make them very durable.

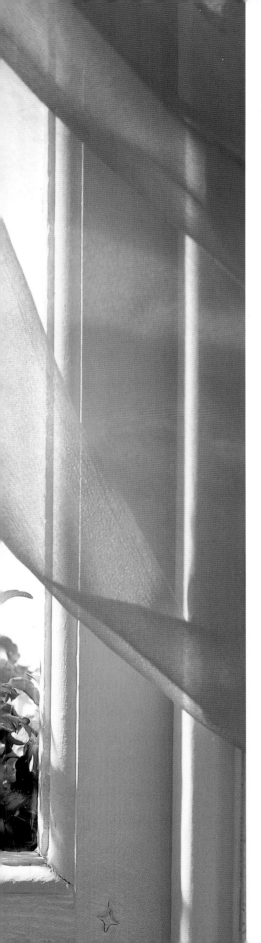

Elephant
Suncatcher

THIS VIBRANT ELEPHANT design was inspired by
the exquisitely detailed embroideries of India. The
rich, warm reds, oranges and purple will shimmer in
the sunshine at your window and throw rainbows
of sumptuous colour into the room. Shisha glass – the
small fragments of mirror that are often sewn onto
fabric – inspired the addition of circles cut from silver
sticky-backed plastic. Gold outliner is used to represent
golden threads and as a finishing touch, the design has
been embellished with shiny sequins. Even when
the sun is not shining, all these glittering
elements will continue to sparkle.

Materials & Equipment

PENCIL

TRACING PAPER

SCISSORS

MASKING TAPE

21½ X 15CM/8½ X 6IN
RECTANGULAR SUNCATCHER

SILVER STICKY-BACKED PLASTIC

GOLD OUTLINER

CRAFT KNIFE

GLASS PAINTS: RED, PURPLE,
DEEP YELLOW, WHITE,
TURQUOISE, ROSE PINK,
BRIGHT PINK AND PALE BLUE

MEDIUM PAINTBRUSH

WHITE CERAMIC TILE,
OLD PLATE OR MIXING TRAY

KITCHEN PAPER

SEQUINS

PVA GLUE

PAIR OF TWEEZERS

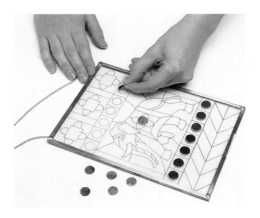

1 Enlarge then trace the template onto tracing paper and cut it out. Tape the tracing under the suncatcher. Cut out 15 circles from silver sticky-backed plastic to fit the circles on the template. Peel the backing paper off the circles and stick them in position on the glass.

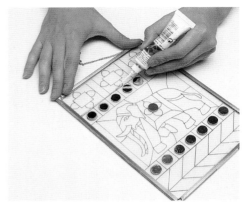

2 Outline the design with gold outliner. Do not apply outliner along the broken lines at this stage. Leave to dry, then remove the tracing. Neaten any irregularities in the lines using a craft knife.

4 Paint the remaining sections on the suncatcher using all the colours except white. Leave to dry.

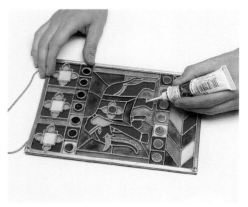

5 Slip the tracing under the glass again and apply dots of outliner along the broken lines.

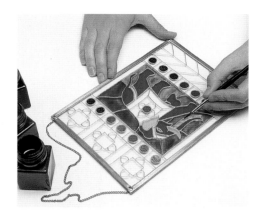

3 Paint the elephant red and its ear, eye and the underside of the trunk deep yellow. Paint the background purple and the tusk white.

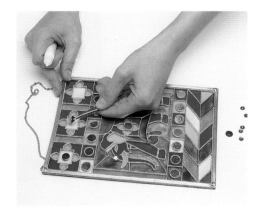

6 To finish, stick sequins to the suncatcher using PVA glue. Use a pair of tweezers to arrange the sequins in position.

Summer Skies Nightlights

SIMPLE GLASS TUMBLERS, votives or small jars containing nightlights make gentle and atmospheric lighting for an alfresco meal on a warm summer evening. Safer and more stable than tall candles, these low-level lights make it much easier to talk to your guests across the table. You could use citronella candles to keep irritating insects at bay, but the butterflies and dragonflies that have been painted flittering across these candle-holders will be lovely and welcome additions to your tablesetting, as their iridescent wings sparkle prettily in the candlelight.

Materials & Equipment

TRACING PAPER

PENCIL

SCISSORS

MASKING TAPE

CLEAR GLASS TUMBLERS,
VOTIVES OR SMALL JARS

KITCHEN PAPER

SILVER OUTLINER

GLASS PAINTS: BRIGHT BLUE,
PALE BLUE, LIME GREEN, JADE,
DEEP YELLOW, GREY AND
COLOURLESS

FINE AND VERY FINE
PAINTBRUSHES

WHITE CERAMIC TILE,
OLD PLATE OR MIXING TRAY

1 Trace an insect motif and cut around it. Tape the tracing inside the glass. If you are making a set of nightlight holders, vary the position of the motif on each one. Lay the glass, with the motif facing up, on a few sheets of kitchen paper to stop it rolling over.

2 Trace the design with silver outliner, applying a steady, even pressure. To draw the delicate antennae, apply the outliner outwards from the motif in short, light strokes so that they taper.

5 When the paint has dried, use a very fine paintbrush to paint jade stripes across the dragonfly's body.

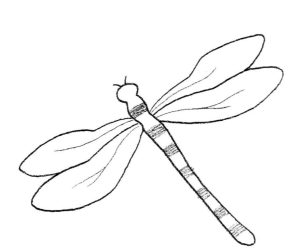

3 Leave the outliner to dry. Pull out the tracing. If necessary, neaten the outline using a craft knife. Paint the butterfly's body grey, then paint the wings using the other colours. As the glass surface is curved, paint only the uppermost areas, then leave to dry before turning the glass to continue.

4 Paint the dragonfly's body lime green. Apply colourless paint to the wings and add pale blue paint close to the body. Blend the paints together.

6 Use the very fine brush to paint delicate veins on the wings in bright blue. Dab any excess paint off the brush to keep the veins as fine as possible.

Christmas Decorations

GIVE YOUR CHRISTMAS tree a touch of
Renaissance opulence with some original
decorations in gorgeous colours, dripping with gold
and jewels. They will glow richly in the Christmas
lights, while the jewels tremble and shimmer. These
fabulously elegant ornaments belie their humble
origins: they can be made very inexpensively, using
off-cuts of acetate and beads from discarded or
broken jewellery. The pendant 'gems' are attached
with headpins, which are available from
craft and bead shops.

Materials & Equipment

TRACING PAPER

PENCIL

MASKING TAPE

ACETATE SHEET

PEARLIZED TEARDROP-SHAPED
JEWELLERY STONE

PVA GLUE

GOLD OUTLINER

KITCHEN PAPER

GLASS PAINTS: DEEP YELLOW
AND OTHER COLOURS TO
CO-ORDINATE WITH THE STONE

FINE PAINTBRUSH

WHITE CERAMIC TILE,
OLD PLATE OR MIXING TRAY

CRAFT KNIFE OR SCISSORS

CUTTING MAT

BRADAWL OR LARGE NEEDLE

THREE PEARL OR GOLD BEADS

THREE GOLD HEADPINS

WIRE CUTTERS OR OLD SCISSORS

ROUND-NOSED PLIERS

FINE GOLD CORD

1 Trace the fleur-de-lys design for the decoration onto tracing paper and tape the tracing under the acetate sheet. Glue the jewellery stone to the centre to make the focal point of the decoration.

2 Set aside for at least 30 minutes for the glue to begin to dry, then run a line of gold outliner around the stone. Draw the rest of the decoration with the outliner, and leave to dry. Remove the tracing.

3 Paint the central parts of the design in deep yellow and paint the teardrops to match the jewellery stone, mixing colours if necessary to create the correct shade. Paint the other areas in a strong colour to set off the stone. Leave to dry.

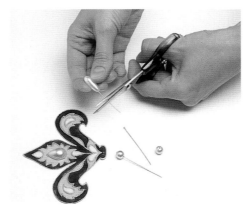

4 Cut out the decoration using a craft knife or a pair of sharp-pointed scissors. You will find that a knife will cut more accurately on the inner angles.

5 Pierce a hole at each marked point using a bradawl or a large needle. Thread each bead onto a headpin. Cut the headpin 1cm/½in above the bead, using wire cutters or an old pair of scissors.

6 Use a small pair of round-nosed pliers to bend the wire above the bead into a loop. Slip the wire loop through a hole on the lower edge of the decoration and close the loop with the pliers. Repeat to suspend the other beads. Hang the decoration on a length of fine gold cord tied through the hole at the top.

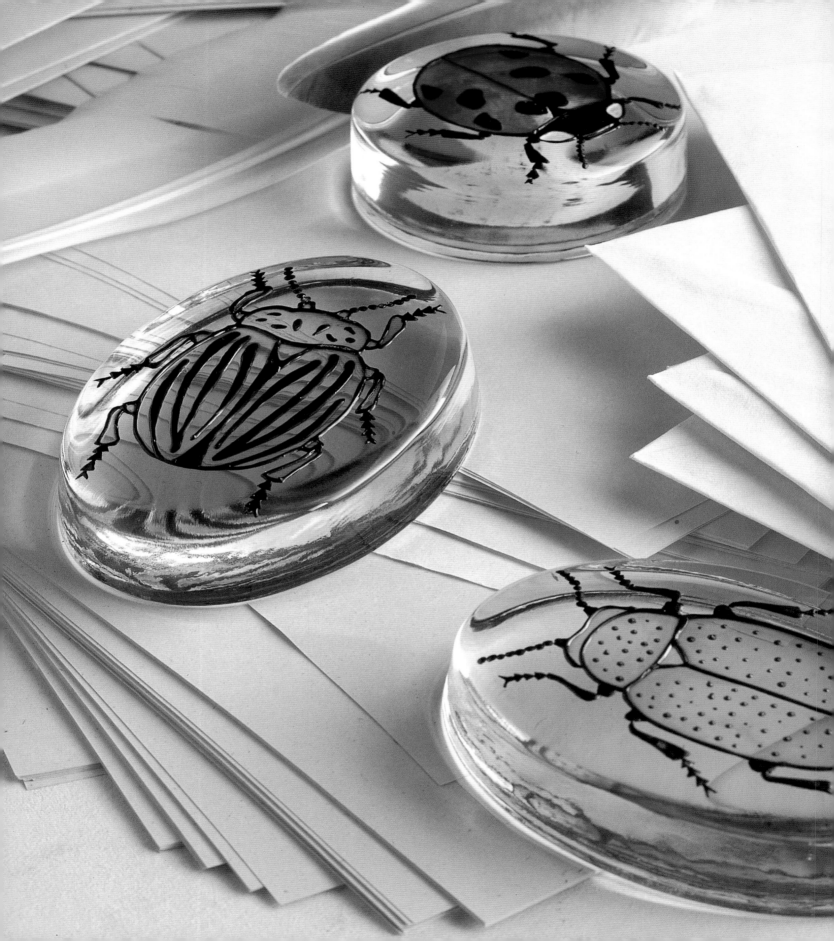

Ugly Bug Paperweights

THE GLOSSY WINGCASES and paintbox colours
of insects make them particularly appropriate
subjects for painted designs on glass. Such creatures
are sure to create a stir, especially when they assume
giant proportions as striking motifs for glass
paperweights. A ladybird, a yellow Colorado beetle
and a green leaf beetle are shown here, but you can
simply change the colours and patterns as you wish to
create your own beastly bugs. Plain glass paperweights
for painting are available from craft suppliers.

Materials & Equipment

TRACING PAPER

PENCIL

CHINAGRAPH PENCIL

MASKING TAPE

GLASS PAPERWEIGHTS

BLACK OUTLINER

GLASS PAINTS: BLACK, WHITE, RED, PINK, DEEP YELLOW, LEMON, BROWN, LIME GREEN, AND COLOURLESS

FINE PAINTBRUSH

WHITE CERAMIC TILE, OLD PLATE OR MIXING TRAY

KITCHEN PAPER

WHITE STICKY-BACKED PLASTIC (OPTIONAL)

SCISSORS

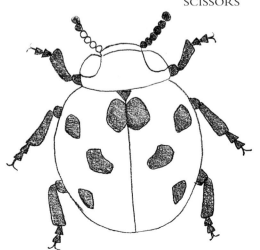

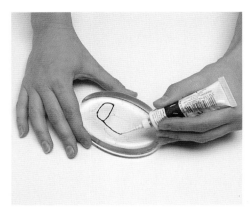

1 The thickness of the paperweight glass makes it difficult to trace through accurately so the image will need to be transferred (see page 13). Trace the insect, then turn the tracing over and draw along the lines using a chinagraph pencil. Do not worry if the chinagraph line is thick and heavy. Turn the tracing over again and tape it to the top of a paperweight. Carefully redraw the insect using a sharp pencil to transfer the design. Remove the tracing.

2 Draw each insect with black outliner. The antennae are rows of dots. Use the outliner to fill in the legs of the ladybird and leaf beetle and the markings on the ladybird and Colorado beetle. Leave to dry.

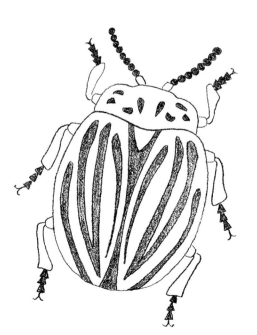

4 Paint the Colorado beetle lemon, adding deep yellow and brown paint around the edges for shading. Paint the whole of each section before moving on to the next to prevent the paint drying before you have finished.

3 Paint the eyes of the ladybird white. Apply colourless paint to the centre of the head and black at each side, then blend the paints together. Apply colourless paint to the wings close to the head. Add a little pink paint, then use red for the rest of the wings, blending the paints together.

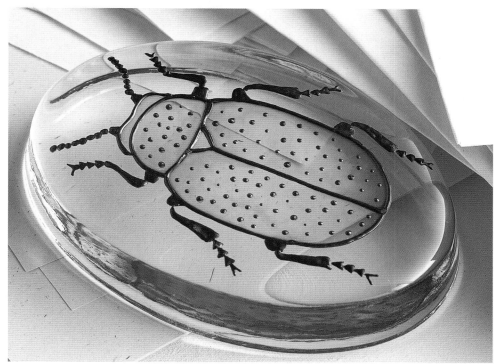

5 Paint the leaf beetle lime green, adding a little brown paint around the edges for shading. Leave to dry then gently dot the insect all over with the outliner. Leave the paperweights to dry.

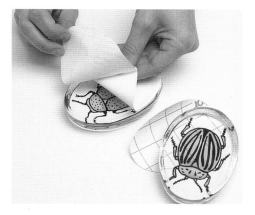

6 If you wish, draw around each paperweight on the paper backing of a piece of sticky-backed plastic. Cut out the shape, cutting 2mm/1/16in inside the outline. Peel off the backing and stick the plastic to the underside of the paperweight.

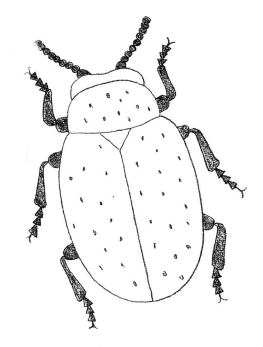

Mosaic Fish Tank

You CAN GIVE any design the appearance of mosaic by simply dividing it into squares or irregular shapes. Since genuine mosaic is made of coloured glass, reproducing the look in outliner and glass paint can be very effective. For this smart fish tank, crystal glass paint was chosen, as it is slightly thicker than other glass paints. Mix a little white paint with the colours to make them more opaque and vary the shade of some of the squares. The white becomes opalescent when dry and resembles the natural changes of colour to be found in the glass tesserae used for real mosaic work.

Materials & Equipment

PENCIL

TRACING PAPER

SCISSORS

MASKING TAPE

14CM/5½IN SQUARE CLEAR
GLASS TANK

PEWTER OUTLINER

CRAFT KNIFE

CRYSTAL GLASS PAINTS: PURPLE,
PINK, YELLOW, BLUE, TURQUOISE,
WHITE AND BLACK

MEDIUM PAINTBRUSH

WHITE CERAMIC TILE,
OLD PLATE OR MIXING TRAY

KITCHEN PAPER

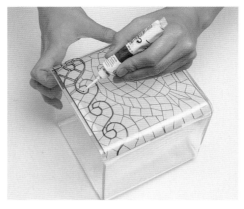

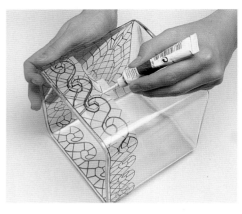

1 Enlarge then trace the template onto tracing paper and cut it out roughly. Tape the tracing inside the front of the tank. Draw the mosaic with the outliner. Leave to dry, then neaten any errors with a craft knife and remove the tracing.

2 Cut off the tracing below the thick lines of the waves. Turn the tank and tape the section under one side, close to the upper edge. Trace the wave with outliner. When dry, outline the waves on the other side and back of the tank. Remove the tracing.

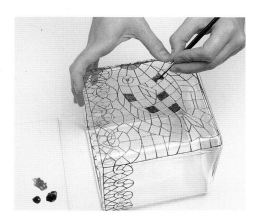

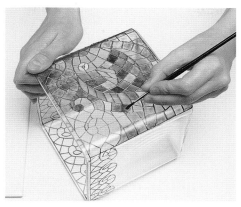

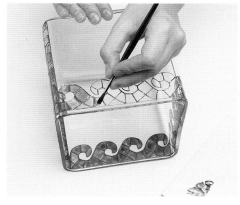

3 Paint the fish, mixing in a little white for some of the squares to vary the shades.

4 Paint the sea blue and the wave border turquoise, again mixing in a little white paint and varying the shades of the squares.

5 Leave to dry, then turn the tank to paint the waves on the sides and back, allowing the paint to dry thoroughly before turning the tank each time.

Greetings Card Menagerie

USE GLASS PAINTS on acetate to make one of these amusing greetings cards for an animal-loving friend. To make it extra special, you could adapt the colouring to resemble their favourite pampered pet. These happy little creatures, all bearing gifts of hearts or flowers, are suspended from the card frames on ribbons, so they can be detached and used as decorations – they would look sweet hanging in a window.

Materials & Equipment

TRACING PAPER

PENCIL

MASKING TAPE

ACETATE SHEET

BLACK OUTLINER

KITCHEN PAPER

GLASS PAINTS: LEMON, DEEP YELLOW, ORANGE, PALE BLUE, GREY, BROWN, RED, PINK, GREEN AND COLOURLESS

FINE PAINTBRUSH

WHITE CERAMIC TILE, OLD PLATE OR MIXING TRAY

CRAFT KNIFE

CUTTING MAT

COLOURED CARD

METAL RULER

WHITE PAPER

PAPER GLUE

BRADAWL OR LARGE NEEDLE

3MM/⅛IN WIDE RIBBON

DOUBLE-SIDED ADHESIVE TAPE

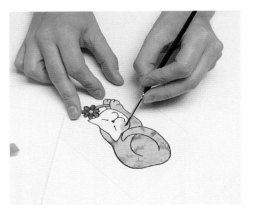

1 Enlarge then trace the animal motif and tape the tracing under the acetate. Draw the animal with black outliner. Leave to dry and remove the tracing.

2 Paint the animal and its gift of hearts or flowers, keeping the area around the facial features light in tone by blending in a little colourless paint. Adding a touch of pink will give a gentle blush. Carefully add stripes and splodges of darker shades, blending the colours together. Finish painting one complete section before moving on to the next. Dot the whiskers on the dog's face using the outliner after the paint has dried. Cut out the motif using a craft knife.

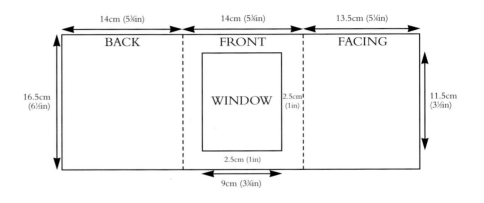

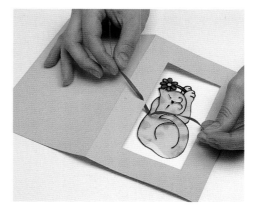

3 Cut a rectangle of coloured card to the dimensions shown in the diagram. Draw the window and fold lines. Cut out the window using a craft knife and a metal ruler. Score and fold along the broken lines.

4 Cut a rectangle of white paper 3mm/⅛in smaller on all edges than the facing. Stick the paper to the underside of the facing.

5 Use a bradawl or a large needle to pierce a hole at the point marked at the top of the animal, and thread with narrow ribbon. Position the animal within the window and pierce a corresponding hole above the window. Thread the ribbon through the hole and tie in a bow. Stick the facing under the front of the card using double-sided tape.

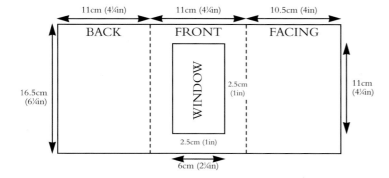

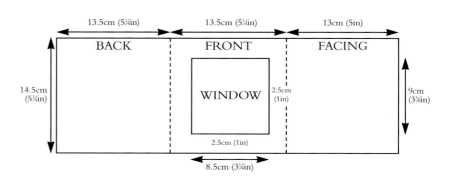

Leaded Mirror

AN ELEGANT STAINED GLASS effect has been

achieved on this mirror by using adhesive lead strip.

The leading is available from craft suppliers and DIY

stores and is easy to apply with the aid of a boning peg,

which is usually supplied with it. The colours used to

paint the mirror have been chosen to tone beautifully

with the cool metallic sheen of the lead. This simple,

bold treatment will turn a cheap, unframed mirror

of any size into a focal point, making a strong colour

accent in a room. If the mirror you have chosen to

decorate has a frame, you could paint it with

metallic paint to match the leading.

Nautical Frame Borders

MAKE A BIGGER splash with your favourite seaside holiday photographs by customizing their frames with stencilled borders of mermaids and shells. Clip frames are cheap and easily available in all sizes, but don't usually add much to the impact of their contents. However, with aptly painted decorations they can make a real contribution.

Remember to choose frames that are large enough to allow generous borders around your pictures: this in itself will enhance the look of the photographs. Before you begin, mount the photographs on cream paper, cut to the size of the frames, by spraying the backs with adhesive then sticking them centrally to the paper and inserting them in the frames. For a really striking effect, match the paint colours with those in your photographs.

Materials & Equipment

TRACING PAPER

PENCIL

STICKY-BACKED PLASTIC

RULER

SCISSORS

MASKING TAPE

CRAFT KNIFE

CUTTING MAT

30 X 25CM/12 X 10IN CLIP
PICTURE FRAME

CERAMIC PAINTS: YELLOW,
ORANGE, BROWN, TURQUOISE,
BLUE AND WHITE

STENCIL BRUSH

WHITE CERAMIC TILE,
OLD PLATE OR MIXING TRAY

KITCHEN PAPER

FINE PAINTBRUSH

1 Trace the template onto tracing paper using a pencil. Cut out two 18 x 8cm/ 7 x 3¼in rectangles of sticky-backed plastic. Tape the tracing face down centrally on the paper backing of the sticky-backed plastic and draw over the lines to transfer the design.

2 Remove the tracing, turn it over and tape it to the other piece of sticky-backed plastic. Transfer the reversed drawing to make a symmetrical design. Remove the tracing and cut out the shapes with a craft knife, resting on a cutting mat.

6 To stencil the mermaid, stick small pieces of masking tape around the cut-outs for the body, face and arms. Mix white with a little red and yellow paint. Stencil the body, face and arms. Allow to dry then peel off the tape. Mask off the areas around the hair. Mix yellow with a little orange paint and stencil the hair.

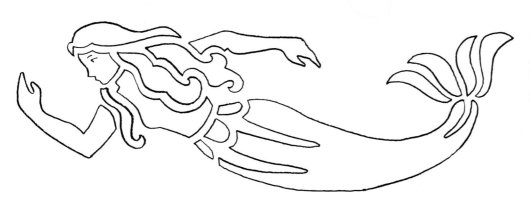

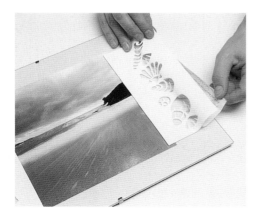

3 Position the stencil on the glass along one edge of the picture. Starting along one long edge of the stencil, carefully peel away the backing paper. Press the stencil smoothly onto the glass.

4 Mix yellow, orange and brown paints together to make a sandy colour for the shells. Dab at the paint with the stencil brush, then, holding the brush upright, apply the paint to the stencil, moving the brush in a circular motion.

5 Leave to dry, then mix brown and a little yellow paint together to make a darker shade. Stick masking tape along the lower edges if you are worried about getting paint on the glass beyond the stencil. Stencil onto the lower edges of the shells. When the paint has dried, mix turquoise and blue with a little white paint. Stencil the shells lightly on their lower edges. Leave the paint to dry, then peel off the stencil.

7 Mask off the cut-outs at the top of the tail. Mix turquoise with a little white paint. Stencil the tail and fin.

8 When the paint has dried, stencil the top of the tail and the fin with blue paint.

9 Use a fine paintbrush to paint the eye and eyebrow carefully on each mermaid. Leave to dry, then peel off the stencils.

Splodge and Swirl Gift Bags

STYLISH GIFT BAGS are a great way to present special gifts, or to turn small gifts into special ones, but are often expensive to buy. It is quite easy to make your own from lightweight acetate, and you can customize it to suit your gift perfectly. Adjust the dimensions shown on the diagram to make the exact size you need.

Three-dimensional gels have been used to decorate these bags and to make the enchanting flower and heart gift tags. Iridescent gel adds a glamorous touch of sparkle. Use a marker pen to write a message on the back of the tag. Wrap your gift in toning tissue to form an ideal background for your painted design, and tie up the package with a chunky raffia bow.

Materials & Equipment

PENCIL

RULER

PLAIN PAPER

LIGHTWEIGHT ACETATE

CHINAGRAPH PENCIL

SCISSORS

PAPERWEIGHT

HOLE PUNCH

TURQUOISE GLASS PAINT

MEDIUM PAINTBRUSH

WHITE CERAMIC TILE,
OLD PLATE OR MIXING TRAY

KITCHEN PAPER

CRYSTAL GEL: BLUE, YELLOW
AND IRIDESCENT

TRACING PAPER

MASKING TAPE

DOUBLE-SIDED ADHESIVE TAPE

BLUE AND YELLOW TISSUE PAPER

RAFFIA

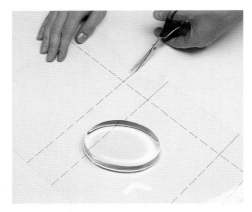 

1 Refer to the diagram to draw a pattern for the bag on plain paper. Lay a sheet of lightweight acetate over the pattern and draw around the outline using a chinagraph pencil. Cut out the bag. Place it on the pattern again and weight it with a heavy object to hold it in place. Cut the slits to the broken lines. Punch holes centrally at the top of the front and back.

2 To make the splodge bag, paint splodges of turquoise glass paint at random between the lines on the front, sides and back of the bag. Set aside to dry. Squeeze blue gel onto a tile, plate or mixing tray. Stir the gel until it has a smooth consistency, then dab it in irregular blobs in the middle of the turquoise painted shapes. Leave to dry.

3 To make the swirl bag, enlarge and trace the templates twice onto tracing paper. Cut them out roughly and tape them to the pattern, matching the broken lines. Place the acetate bag on top and weight it with a heavy object.

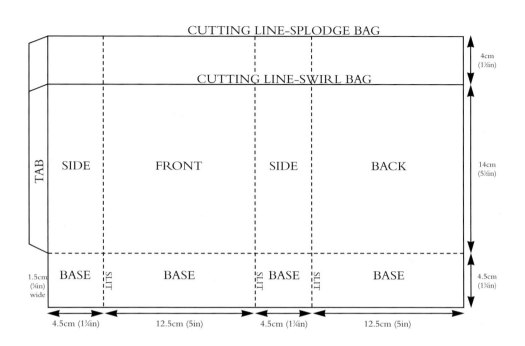

CUTTING LINE-SPLODGE BAG

4cm (1½in)

CUTTING LINE-SWIRL BAG

| TAB | SIDE | FRONT | SIDE | BACK |

14cm (5½in)

| BASE | SLIT | BASE | SLIT | BASE | SLIT | BASE |

1.5cm (⅝in) wide

4.5cm (1¾in)

4.5cm (1¾in) 12.5cm (5in) 4.5cm (1¾in) 12.5cm (5in)

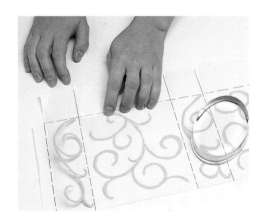

4 Squeeze out some yellow gel and stir until it has a smooth consistency, then paint it onto the acetate along the 'swirls'. Leave to dry then remove the pattern. Turn the pattern over and redraw the lines on the other side. Place the bag face down on the pattern and hold it in place with a weight. Using the pattern as a guide, fold the bag along the fold lines. Stick the tab under the back using double-sided tape.

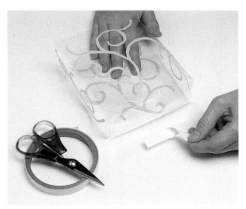

5 Tuck the short sides of the base inside then fold under the long sides and stick them together using double-sided tape. Wrap the gift in tissue paper and slip it into the bag. Tuck in the sides of the bag at the top and fasten with lengths of raffia, threaded through the punched holes and tied in a bow.

6 To make the gift tags, trace the flower or heart onto tracing paper. Tape the tracing under a piece of acetate. Squeeze out the gels and add some iridescent gel to the yellow. Stir the gels until they have a smooth consistency then paint them thickly within the outlines. Leave to dry, then peel the paint off the acetate. Make a hole in the top with a scissor point for hanging. Thread a length of raffia through the hole. Tie the tag to the raffia bow.

Recycled Glass Candle-holders

MANY GLASS CONTAINERS can be recycled, and look very attractive serving a purpose other than that for which they were originally intended. Here, a jam jar and a couple of odd glasses – a sherry glass and a shot glass – have been given a new lease of life as pretty candle-holders. Although the shapes are mismatched, the use of co-ordinating motifs and the same range of colours has turned them into a matching set. The screw thread on the jar has been prettily disguised with a twist of gold cord, trimmed with glass beads decorated with gold outliner.

Materials & Equipment

PENCIL

TRACING PAPER

SCISSORS

MASKING TAPE

CLEAR GLASS JAM JAR,
SHERRY AND SHOT GLASSES

GOLD OUTLINER

CRAFT KNIFE

GLASS PAINTS: BRIGHT PINK, DEEP
YELLOW AND TURQUOISE

MEDIUM AND FINE PAINTBRUSHES

WHITE CERAMIC TILE,
OLD PLATE OR MIXING TRAY

KITCHEN PAPER

GOLD CORD

TWO TURQUOISE BEADS
WITH LARGE HOLES

ADHESIVE TAPE

COTTON BUD

1 Trace the templates onto tracing paper and cut them out roughly. Tape the large round motif inside the jar. Outline the design with gold outliner. Leave to dry then remove the tracing. Neaten any errors in the outlines using a craft knife.

2 Paint the jar, using a fine paintbrush to work the paint into the tight corners. Set the jar aside to dry. Check that the cord is narrow enough to thread through the beads. Wrap adhesive tape tightly around the cord end and cut it to a point to ease it through the hole if necessary.

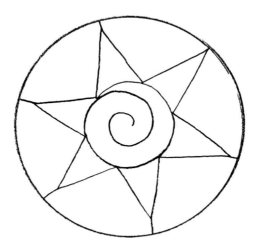

6 Paint the band and the stem. Set aside to dry, then stand the glass upright to paint the base. Leave to dry, then dot the base with outliner.

3 Tie the cord around the screw thread on the jar. Cut one end off a cotton bud and slip a bead onto the cut end. Dot with gold outliner and leave to dry; decorate the other bead in the same way. Thread the beads onto the cord ends. Knot the ends under the beads and cut off the excess cord.

4 To position the band on the sherry glass, fill the glass with water to the point where you want the lower line and stand it on a level surface. Trace along the line with gold outliner. Add more water to raise the level by 2cm/¾in and trace the second line in the same way.

5 Leave the outliner to dry, then tip away the water and dry the glass thoroughly. Make five tracings of the spiral and tape them, evenly spaced, inside the glass between the lines. Resting the glass on kitchen paper for support, trace the spirals with gold outliner then apply bands of outliner around the stem, following the moulding of the glass. Leave to dry.

7 Make a few tracings of the small star and tape them at random inside the shot glass. Resting the glass on kitchen paper, trace the stars with outliner. The faceted base of this glass was also edged with outliner. Allow to dry, then paint the glass.

Floral Flasks

THESE THREE PRETTY BOTTLES for the bathroom

shelf have each been decorated using a different

technique but, standing together, their distinctive styles

harmonize perfectly with each other. The tall, frosted

bottle is randomly painted with flowers using colourless

paint, which turns the frosted surface transparent. The

square bottle has a delicately painted fritillary set within

a silver frame, and its cork stopper, which was originally

plain, has been cleverly trimmed with glass beads. The

small bottle is dotted with pink hydrangea florets. Any

or all of them would make a lovely gift, filled with

delicious, floral-scented bath salts or essences.

Materials & Equipment

FROSTED, SMALL CLEAR AND
SQUARE-SIDED, CORKED BOTTLES

GLASS PAINTS: COLOURLESS,
WHITE, BRIGHT PINK,
TURQUOISE AND GREY

MEDIUM AND FINE PAINTBRUSHES

FROSTING MEDIUM

WHITE CERAMIC TILE,
OLD PLATE OR MIXING TRAY

KITCHEN PAPER

TRACING PAPER

PENCIL

PLAIN PAPER

SCISSORS

CHINAGRAPH PENCIL

SILVER OUTLINER

CRAFT KNIFE

LARGE PEARL-HEADED PIN

ONE CLEAR GLASS ROUND
AND ONE DISC BEAD

WIRE CUTTERS

SUPERGLUE

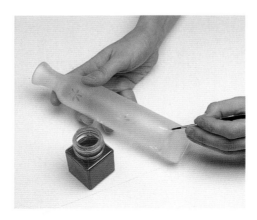

1 To apply the flowers to the frosted bottle, use colourless paint to paint a dot, then paint six petals radiating outwards with single brush strokes. Apply the flowers at random all over the bottle.

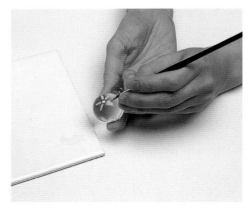

2 Paint flowers on a clear glass stopper with white paint mixed with frosting medium. Follow the manufacturer's instructions, as some frosting mediums are not mixed with the paint but applied separately after the paint has dried.

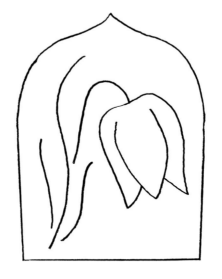

6 Mix turquoise with colourless paint to lighten the colour. Refer to the template to paint the stem and leaves of the fritillary, using a fine paintbrush, to the left of the framed area.

3 To paint the hydrangea florets on the small bottle, first mix white with a little bright pink paint. Resting the bottle on kitchen paper, paint a small cross, then paint a petal on each arm of the cross. Add a little bright pink paint at the base of each petal and stroke it outwards along the petal. Paint the florets at random on the uppermost section of the bottle. Leave to dry, then turn the bottle to continue painting.

4 When the florets are dry, mix white and bright pink paint together. Use a fine paintbrush to paint a few veins on each petal. Dot the flower centres.

5 For the square bottle, trace the frame template and cut it out. Resting on a few sheets of kitchen paper, hold the template on the bottle and draw around it with a chinagraph pencil. Remove the template and trace along the drawn line with silver outliner, adding small curls at the corners. Allow to dry.

7 Mix grey with colourless paint and paint the outline of the flower. Mix bright pink with colourless paint. Apply a checkered pattern on the flower with single dabs of a fine paintbrush. Mix in a little more colourless paint for the checks across the centre of the flower to lighten the colour. Mix grey into the colour to paint the rear petals visible at the lower edge. Set aside to dry.

8 Use a craft knife to cut off the top of the cork so it does not stand too far proud of the bottle. Thread the pin through the round bead, then through the disc bead. Snip off the pin 1cm/½in below the beads with wire cutters. Dab superglue on the end of the pin and push it into the centre of the cork.

Mediterranean Oil Bottles

THE DECORATIONS on these cooking oil bottles identify their contents with pictorial labels that glow with southern sunshine. This trio would make a wonderful gift – especially if you have added your own flavourings to the oil – although you may be tempted to keep them yourself. As the oil in the bottles is quite dark, pale squares and circles are stencilled first to provide a clear background to paint on. The stencilled circles have been turned into orange slices, but depending on the flavourings in your oil you might want to make these lemon or lime slices instead. The bottle with one square motif has a beaming sunflower and the one with three squares has a selection of enticing herbs.

Materials & Equipment

STICKY-BACKED PLASTIC

PENCIL

RULER

SCISSORS

SQUARE-SIDED BOTTLES
OF FLAVOURED OIL

MASKING TAPE

GLASS PAINTS: WHITE, LEMON
YELLOW, ORANGE, GREEN,
BROWN AND PALE BLUE

FLAT, MEDIUM AND FINE
PAINTBRUSHES

WHITE CERAMIC TILE,
OLD PLATE OR MIXING TRAY

KITCHEN PAPER

CHINAGRAPH PENCIL

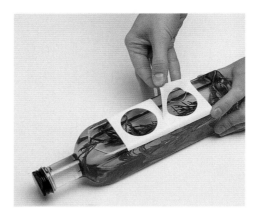

1 For the bottle with circular motifs, cut two 6cm/2½in squares of sticky-backed plastic to use as stencils. Cut out a 4cm/1½in circle in the centre of each square. Peel off the backing paper and stick to the front of the bottle.

2 Using masking tape, mask off a 4cm/1½in square on the front of the sunflower and herb bottles. Mask off two more 4cm/1½in squares above and below this on the herb bottle.

5 Use a chinagraph pencil to mark the glass around the orange slices, dividing each into eight sections. Paint an orange segment within each division. Wipe away the pencil marks when the paint has dried.

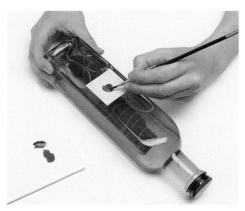

6 Paint an orange circle on the centre of the sunflower square about 1cm/½in in diameter. Before the paint dries, paint a brown ring around the circumference.

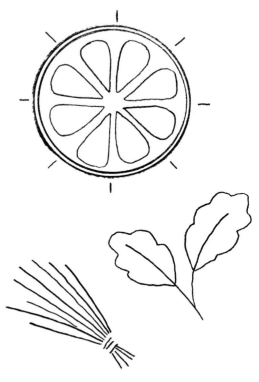

3 Mix white with a little lemon yellow paint to make a creamy colour. Paint the circles and squares, applying the paint quite thickly to give a dense covering. Leave to dry.

4 Paint the rind on the orange slices about 3mm/⅛in wide around the circumference of the circles, using orange paint. Leave to dry. Peel off the sticky-backed plastic and masking tape on the bottles.

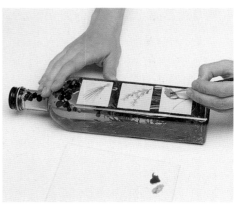

7 Paint the petals with lemon yellow paint, using a single brush stroke for each petal, radiating outwards from the circle. While the paint is still wet, use a fine paintbrush to paint a deep yellow line on each petal, radiating outwards from the centre of the sunflower.

8 For the herb bottle, paint a bunch of chives in the top square, applying single brush strokes of green with a fine paint-brush. Paint three strokes of brown to represent string tying the chives. Paint two brown stems on the middle square for a sprig of rosemary. Paint green leaves then dot with pale blue paint for the buds.

9 Finally, in the lower square, paint two green stems with a large green leaf on each for lemon balm. Blend in a little lemon yellow paint at the tip of the leaves.

Pastel
Petal Box

WHITE GLASS PAINT mixed into a range of pretty

colours makes opaque, sugared-almond shades to

decorate a glass-sided box – this one has a silvery lid and

base that suggest the cool colour scheme, but the style

would suit any square-sided container. The finished box

shows the interesting effects that can be achieved by

applying glass paint in several layers, allowing each to dry

before painting the next. The petals are applied using two

stamps, easily made from foam. Paint the outlines and

accents with a confident hand for a lively, spontaneous

effect. The freehand style results in a design of great

panache, giving a novel edge to its delicate colouring.

Materials & Equipment

GLASS PAINTS: WHITE, VIOLET,
TURQUOISE, PALE BLUE
AND BRIGHT PINK

FLAT AND FINE PAINTBRUSHES

WHITE CERAMIC TILE,
OLD PLATE OR MIXING TRAY

CLEAR GLASS BOX

TAPE REEL

KITCHEN PAPER

SILVER CERAMIC PAINT

TRACING PAPER

PENCIL

SCISSORS

NEOPRENE FOAM

CRAFT KNIFE (OPTIONAL)

CORRUGATED CARD

ALL-PURPOSE HOUSEHOLD GLUE

1 Mix white and violet paint together. With the box face up and supported as necessary, use a flat paintbrush to paint a vertical band 2cm/³⁄₄in wide down each side. Mix white and turquoise paint together and paint a 5cm/2in wide band in the centre.

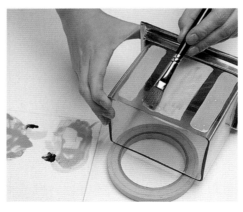

2 Use silver ceramic paint and a fine paintbrush to add a row of diagonal dashes between the bands. When the paint has dried, paint a silver dot in the centre of the middle band.

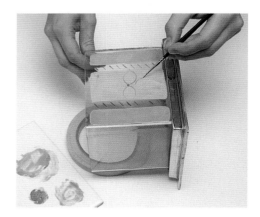

6 Mix violet with white paint. Use a fine paintbrush to outline the central petals, then mix bright pink and white paint together to outline the outer petals. Use the other colours mixed with white to paint veins on the petals and to apply random brush strokes to the central band.

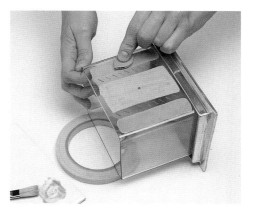

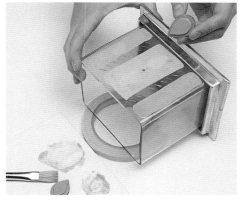

3 To make the stamps, draw the two petals on paper. Cut out and draw around the templates on the foam. Cut out the shapes with a craft knife or a pair of scissors. Glue the foam petals firmly onto the corrugated card using all-purpose glue. Cut the card around the foam shapes, leaving a 5mm/¼in wide border.

4 Mix pale blue with white paint and paint it onto the small petal stamp. Press the stamp diagonally onto the top then the bottom of one outer band. Repeat midway between the first two petals, then stamp the other outer band in the same way. Wipe the stamp clean.

5 Mix bright pink with white paint. Paint onto the large petal stamp and apply vertically to the top and bottom of the middle band, radiating out from the dot. Use the small petal stamp to apply small pink petals horizontally at each side of the dot. Clean the stamp.

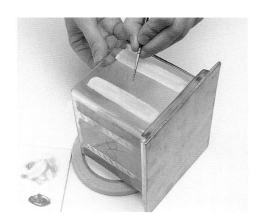

7 Leave the front of the box to dry, then paint a co-ordinating design on the sides, applying bands of pale blue mixed with white and stamping them with the small petals. Add dashes of silver between the bands as before.

Frosted Leaf Vase

A SINGLE LARGE LEAF in a beautiful soft blue decorates this icy-green, frosted glass vase. Crackle glaze has been applied to the painted leaf, and the cracks resemble the fine veins to be found on skeletal leaves. Adding white paint to the blue gives it an opacity which effectively matches the frosting on the glass, and no outline has been used for the motif. The result is stylish and bold, with an oriental feel – perfect for a modern setting and a long way from conventional painted glass designs. Make sure you choose a crackle glaze that is compatible with the paints you use. Read the manufacturer's instructions carefully before you begin, and experiment with the combination on a piece of spare glass first to test the technique.

Materials & Equipment

TRACING PAPER

PENCIL

SCISSORS

MASKING TAPE

PALE GREEN, FROSTED GLASS VASE

CARTRIDGE PAPER (OPTIONAL)

KITCHEN PAPER

GLASS PAINT: TURQUOISE
AND WHITE

WHITE CERAMIC TILE,
OLD PLATE OR MIXING TRAY

MEDIUM AND FINE PAINTBRUSHES

CRACKLE GLAZE

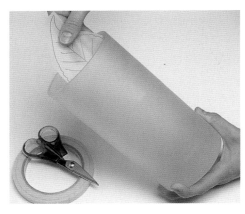

1 Trace the template onto tracing paper and cut it out roughly. Stick the template inside the vase. If the tracing is not visible through the glass, cut the shape out of cartridge paper and tape it to the outside of the vase, then lightly draw around it with a sharp pencil.

2 Lay the vase, leaf side uppermost, on a few sheets of kitchen paper to stop it rolling. Mix turquoise and white paint together and paint the leaf. If your vase is deeply rounded, as this one is, start by painting just one half of the leaf – up to the central vein. Allow to dry, then turn the vase to paint the other half. Set aside to dry completely and remove the template.

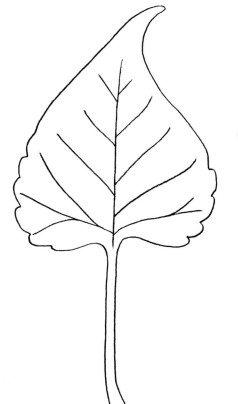

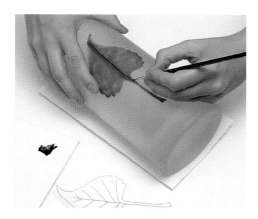

3 Referring to the template, paint the central vein turquoise, using a fine paintbrush.

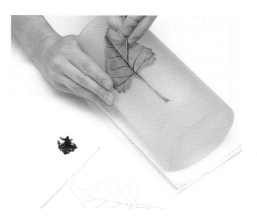

4 Paint the smaller veins radiating out from the central vein in the same way, and leave to dry.

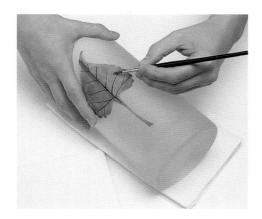

5 Paint the leaf with crackle glaze and set aside to dry. Fine cracks will gradually appear on the surface. The process can be hastened by holding a hair dryer, on a cool setting, over the crackle glaze to dry it.

Filigree Candle Shade

As well as looking decorative, candle shades serve a useful purpose in diffusing the light and shielding the flame from draughts. This pure white frosted shade will maximize the light, at the same time turning it into a gentle glow. A delicate filigree border adds an exquisitely pretty embellishment, glinting with silver highlights and showing up in silhouette when lit from within. The design is painted with pewter ceramic paint to co-ordinate with the metal candlestick. Silver outliner has been used to add small points of raised decoration as a finishing touch. If you would prefer a bolder look, you could use outliner to draw the entire border.

Materials & Equipment

WHITE FROSTED CANDLE SHADE

TRACING PAPER

MASKING TAPE

SHARP AND SOFT PENCILS

RULER

SCISSORS

FINE PAINTBRUSH

PEWTER CERAMIC PAINT

WHITE CERAMIC TILE,
OLD PLATE OR MIXING TRAY

KITCHEN PAPER

SILVER OUTLINER

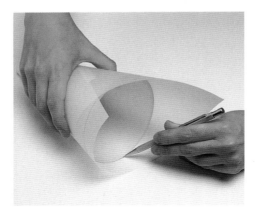

1 To make a pattern, lay the shade centrally on a piece of tracing paper. Wrap the paper over the shade and tape it in place. Draw along the top and bottom edges of the shade on the paper. Mark the position where the edges of the paper overlap at the top and bottom.

2 Undo the tape, remove the shade and join the overlap marks with a ruler. Cut out the pattern.

3 Using a soft pencil, enlarge and trace the template onto the lower edge of the pattern. Tape the pattern, pencil side down, smoothly around the shade, matching the broken lines to the lower edge of the shade. Redraw the design firmly, using a sharp pencil to transfer it to the shade.

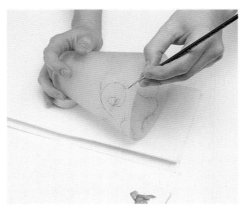

4 Remove the tracing. Using a fine paintbrush, paint the design on the shade with pewter ceramic paint. Leave each section to dry as you complete it, so you do not smudge the painted areas when you turn the shade.

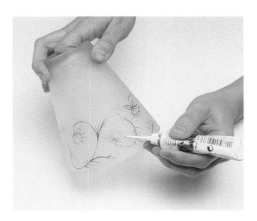

5 Apply silver outliner to the dots. Take care to keep these small to maintain the delicate look of the piece.

Seafarer's Lantern

GLASS-SIDED LANTERNS make pretty, portable

lighting for the garden, and attractive decorations even

when they are not in use. The cool, bleached blue tones

of the wooden frame around this smart lantern

suggested a nautical theme for its painted panels.

Pewter outliner was used to match the metalwork and

enhance the colour scheme, but choose an outliner that

will go well with your own lantern: for instance, gold

would look good on a brass lantern, or one with brass

fittings. If you are buying a lantern to decorate, look

for one with removable glass panels if possible,

as they will be much easier to paint.

Materials & Equipment

LANTERN

RULER

PENCIL

TRACING PAPER

MASKING TAPE

PEWTER OUTLINER

CRAFT KNIFE

GLASS PAINTS: BRIGHT BLUE, PALE BLUE AND COLOURLESS

FINE PAINTBRUSH

WHITE CERAMIC TILE, OLD PLATE OR MIXING TRAY

KITCHEN PAPER

1 Remove the glass panes from the lantern if possible. Measure the panes and draw two panels to size on tracing paper, one for the front and the other for the two sides. Trace the motifs onto the panels, placing a rope border at the top and bottom of each one. When you are happy with the designs, tape them under the glass. Trace the motifs with the outliner and leave to dry.

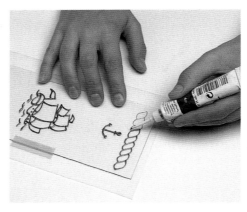

2 Remove the tracings. Make neat points on the anchors by cutting through the outliner across the tips using a craft knife. Pull away the tiny pieces you have cut off. Neaten any other heavy blobs of outliner with the craft knife in the same way.

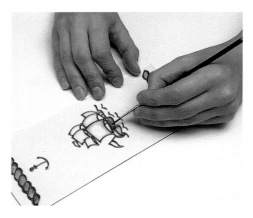

5 Paint the side of the ship and the flags pale blue, then add bright blue paint and blend the colours together.

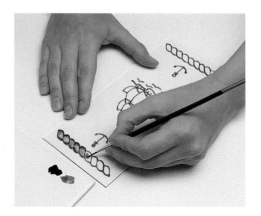

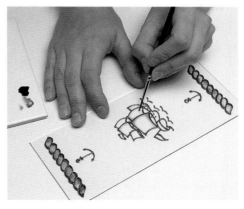

3 Paint the rope borders pale blue and add bright blue paint along the upper and lower edges for shading. Paint the compass points and centre bright blue and pale blue in alternate panels.

4 Paint the sails with colourless paint. Add pale blue paint around the edges and blend the paints together.

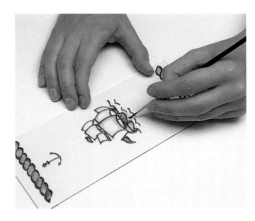

6 Apply colourless paint to the tips of the waves. Gradually blend in a little pale blue and bright blue paint for the sea. Do not apply the paint too thickly here as it is not contained within an outline: allow it to thin out gradually and become paler, so that there is no hard edge. Leave the paint to dry, then assemble the lantern.

Tortoiseshell Vase

THE BEAUTIFUL WARM colours and abstract patterns of tortoiseshell not only turned it into a precious commodity but also provided inspiration for many varied, decorative effects. Both glass and plastic, being fluid, transparent materials, can be manufactured incorporating patterns that resemble tortoiseshell, but it is also possible to produce a fine imitation of this lovely effect with paint, using a simple sponging technique. A large, natural sponge gives the right degree of random mottling on this striking vase. The first step is to paint the vase all over: any streaks and irregularities in this background painting are disguised by the sponging.

Materials & Equipment

CLEAR GLASS VASE

TAPE REEL

GLASS PAINTS: VERMILION, BROWN AND DEEP BROWN

FLAT PAINTBRUSH

WHITE CERAMIC TILE OR OLD PLATE

NATURAL SPONGE

WHITE SPIRIT OR WATER

1 Stand the vase on a small, flat object such as a tape reel so the wet paint does not come into contact with another surface. Paint the outside of the vase all over with vermilion paint, using a flat paintbrush. Work as quickly and evenly as possible, so the paint does not start to dry before you have finished.

2 Lightly moisten a natural sponge, using white spirit if you are using oil-based paints, or water for water-based paints. Using a flat paintbrush, apply an even layer of brown paint to a tile or an old plate.

4 Apply deep brown paint to the tile using the flat paintbrush. Dab at the paint with the sponge. (There is no need to clean the sponge between colours.)

3 Dab at the paint with the sponge and apply randomly all over the vase.

5 Now dab the deep brown paint all over the vase. Hold the vase up to the light to check for any areas you may have missed, and sponge those too. Clean the sponge immediately so the paint does not stain it.

Index

ACKNOWLEDGEMENTS

The author and publishers would like to thank
Framecraft Miniatures Ltd, Forbo Mayfair Ltd,
and 3M UK plc for supplying materials for this book.

RESOURCES

DMC Creative World Ltd
Pullman Road
Wigton
Leicestershire LE18 2DY
Tel: 0116 281 1040
*(glass painting kits; contact
for your nearest stockist)*

Forbo CP Ltd
Station Road
Cramlington
Northumberland NE23 8AQ
Tel: 01670 718300
*(Fablon sticky-backed plastic;
contact for your nearest stockist)*

Framecraft Miniatures Ltd
372-376 Summer Lane
Hockley
Birmingham B19 3QA
Tel: 0121 212 0551
*(glass paperweights; mail
order available)*

Fred Aldous
PO Box 135
37 Lever Street
Manchester 1
M60 1UX
Tel: 0161 236 2477
*(glass paperweights and
suncatchers; mail order available)*

Homecrafts Direct
PO Box 38
Leicester LE1 9BU
Tel: 0116 251 3139
*(paints, leading and glass items;
mail order available)*

Philip & Tacey Ltd
North Way
Andover
Hampshire SP10 5BA
Tel: 01264 332171
*(suppliers of Pebeo glass paints
and outliner; contact for your
nearest stockist)*

3M UK plc
3M House
Market Place
Bracknell RG12 1JU
Tel: 01344 858000
*(stencil mount; contact for
your nearest stockist)*